Let's Learn About

LITERATURE

# PICTURE BOOKS

Heather
Moore Niver

**Enslow Publishing**
101 W. 23rd Street
Suite 240
New York, NY 10011
USA

enslow.com

# WORDS TO KNOW

**author**  A person who writes.

**characters**  People in stories, plays, movies, or other works of literature.

**collage**  A kind of art made from all kinds of different things.

**fiction**  A story that is made up.

**illustration**  A picture in a book.

**illustrator**  A person who draws pictures for a book.

**medium**  Material used to create art.

**nonfiction**  A story based on facts.

**setting**  The place where a story happens.

**spread**  Two pages facing each other in a book.

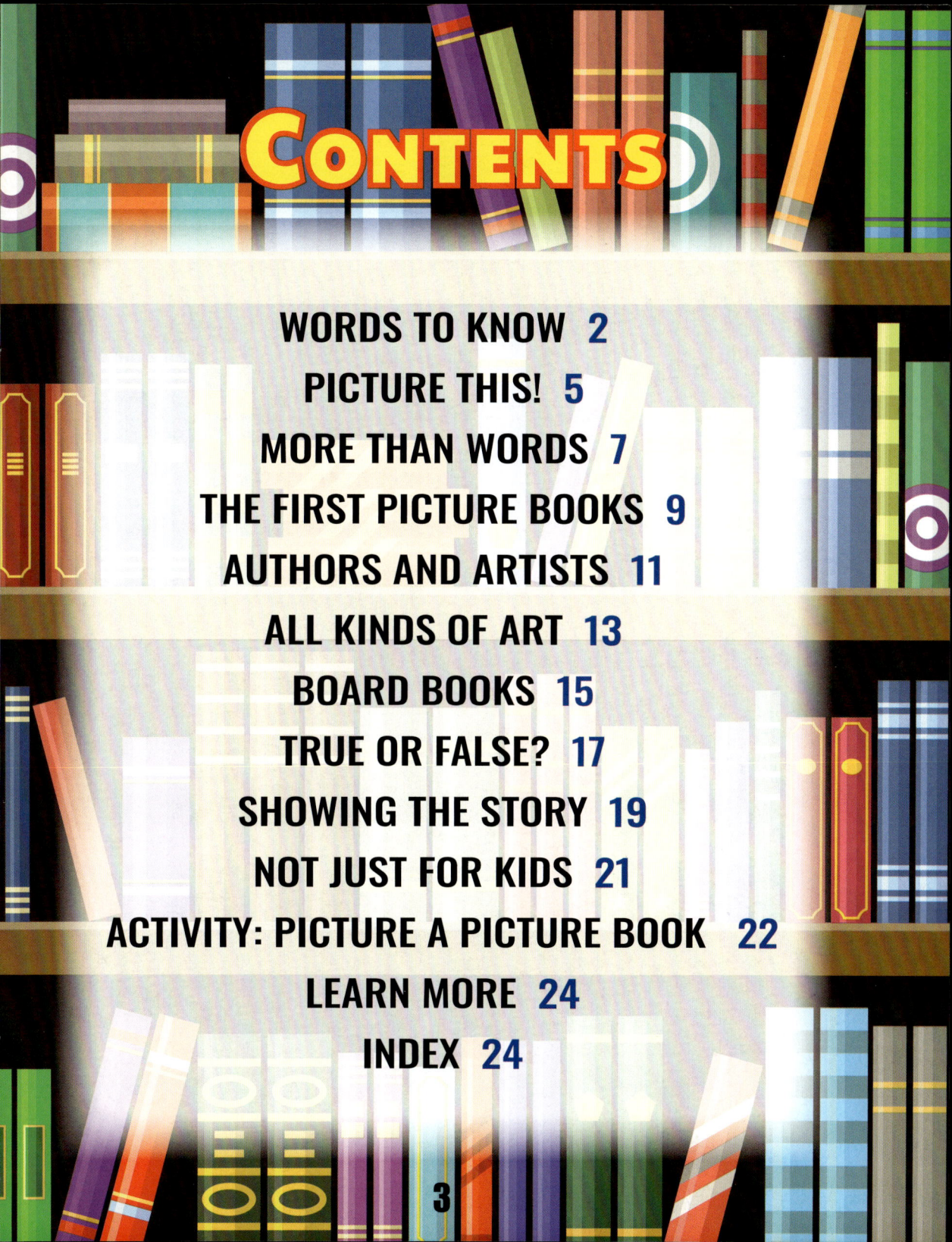

# Contents

Picture books use illustrations to help tell a story.

# Picture This!

A picture book tells a story. It has many **illustrations**. A picture book usually has words, too, but not always!

## FAST FACT

A picture book has an illustration on every page or **spread**.

A scene from *The Snowman*. This book has no words.

# More Than Words

Wordless picture books tell stories just by using illustrations. Raymond Briggs's *The Snowman* is a well-known story. He only uses pictures.

## FAST FACT

Most picture books are 32 pages long. Some have only 24 pages.

A very old copy of a Peter Rabbit
book. Peter is a naughty rabbit
who gets in lots of trouble.

# The Tale of
# PETER RABBIT.

## By BEATRIX POTTER.

# The First Picture Books

Picture books have been around for a long time. The first ones appeared in the late 1800s. Beatrix Potter wrote her famous books about Peter Rabbit around this time.

## Fast Fact

**Picture books began as a fun way to teach kids how to read.**

Dr. Seuss works on the drawings for one of his books.

# Authors and Artists

The **author** writes the story. Sometimes the author illustrates his own book. Other times an author and artist both work on a book. The artist, or **illustrator**, creates the story's pictures.

**FAST FACT**

Dr. Seuss wrote and illustrated almost all of his books himself.

**Artists work hard to find the medium that will work best for a picture book.**

# All Kinds of Art

The illustrations in a picture book are often bright. They are colorful. They can be made with almost any **medium** you can imagine. Artists use paints, pens, pencils, computers, and more.

## FAST FACT

Artists sometimes use all kinds of materials, or **collage**, in picture books.

Board books
are great for
babies because
they can't rip
the pages!

# Board Books

Babies start out looking at board books. These are very short books with thick pages. They have simple words and bright pictures. Perfect for the youngest readers!

Both fiction and nonfiction books use illustrations to show the reader what the book is about.

# True or False?

Picture books can be about anything. For example, some stories are made up. These are called **fiction**. Other stories are based on facts. These **nonfiction** tales are true.

In Maurice Sendak's *Where the Wild Things Are*, the setting changes from a boy's bedroom to a jungle.

# Showing the Story

The artist's pictures should help tell the story. Sometimes they show the **setting**, or where the story happens. The illustrations also show the **characters** in the book.

## FAST FACT

Each year, the Caldecott Medal is awarded to the best American picture book.

**Author Brian Selznick talks about one of his drawings for *Hugo Cabret.***

# Not Just for Kids

Most people think picture books are for kids. *The Invention of Hugo Cabret* was written by Brian Selznick. It has 525 pages! The pictures help tell the story.

**FUN FACT**

**More than 280 pages in *The Invention of Hugo Cabret* have illustrations.**

# Activity

## Picture a Picture Book

**MATERIALS**
- picture books
- paper
- colored pencils
- magazines

The pictures in a picture book are what make it so special. You can make your very own picture book!

Choose your favorite picture book. What colors does it use?

What is the artwork like? Is it soft and dreamy? Is it bold and exciting?

Think about a story you might like to write. One idea is to write about your favorite funny family story. Or make something up!

Create the cover for your book, either by drawing it or creating a collage of pictures cut out of magazines.

You can use the colors and styles of your favorite book or do something all your own!

# LEARN MORE

## Books

Giff, Patricia Riley. *Writing with Rosie: You Can Write a Story Too*. New York, NY: Holiday House, 2016.

Holub, Joan, and Melissa Sweet. *Little Red Writing*. San Francisco, CA: Chronicle Books LLC, 2016.

Lehrhaupt, Adam, and Magali Le Huche. *This Is a Good Story*. New York, NY: Simon & Schuster Books for Young Readers, 2017.

## Websites

### Kids Buzz
*kidsbuzz.prattlibrary.org/read/?tpc=main*
Search for picture books of all kinds on this website.

### Picture Prompts
*kidsarewriters.com/tag/picture-prompts/*
Check out this page to get ideas for writing your own stories!

# INDEX

Published in 2019 by Enslow Publishing, LLC.
101 W. 23rd Street, Suite 240, New York, NY 10011

Copyright © 2019 by Enslow Publishing, LLC.

All rights reserved.

No part of this book may be reproduced by any means without the written permission of the publisher.

**Library of Congress Cataloging-in-Publication Data**

Names: Niver, Heather Moore, author.
Title: Picture books / Heather Moore Niver.
Description: New York, NY : Enslow Publishing, LLC., [2019] | Series: Let's learn about literature | Audience: K-4 |Includes bibliographical references and index.
Identifiers: LCCN 2017045221| ISBN 9780766097476 (library bound) | ISBN 9780766097483 (softcover) | ISBN 9780766097490 (6 pack)
Subjects: LCSH: Picture books—Study and teaching (Elementary) | Picture books for children—Study and teaching (Elementary) | Picture books—Juvenile literature. | Literary form—Juvenile literature. |Language arts (Elementary)
Classification: LCC PN3427 .N586 2019 | DDC 096/.1—dc23
LC record available at https://lccn.loc.gov/2017045221

Printed in the United States of America

**To Our Readers**: We have done our best to make sure all website addresses in this book were active and appropriate when we went to press. However, the author and the publisher have no control over and assume no liability for the material available on those websites or on any websites they may link to. Any comments or suggestions can be sent by e-mail to customerservice@enslow.com.

**Photo Credits:** Cover, p. 1 Len44ik/Shutterstock.com; pp. 2–3, 24 Gurza/Shutterstock.com; p. 4 Samuel Borges Photography/Shutterstock.com; pp. 5, 7, 9, 11, 13, 15, 17, 19, 21, 22–23 (paper, notebook, pencil) narmacero/Shutterstock.com; pp. 5, 7, 11, 15, 17, 19, 21, 22 (open book) Wen Wen/Shutterstock.com; p. 6 Dan Kitwood/Getty Images; p. 8 Carl Court/Getty Images; p. 10 James L. Amos/Corbis Historical/Getty Images; p. 12 Mostovyi Sergii Igorevich/Shutterstock.com; p. 14 Kimberly Hall/Shutterstock.com; p. 16 moodboard/Alamy Stock Photo; p. 18 Richard Levine/Alamy Stock Photo; p. 20 Ernesto S. Ruscio/Getty Images; p. 22 Evgeny Hmur/Shutterstock.com.